Garden of Words weaves together the art and poetry of Pnina Granirer in a testament to an incredible life lived. One shaped, weathered, etched, and eroded by forces far greater than ourselves, much like the enigmatic landscape of Gabriola Island where the artist found much solace and inspiration. From the outset her poetry serves as the warp holding tension and the framework of her life, while her visual art acts as the weft, drawn through, over and under the warp to turn these threads into the fabric which defines her life. Pnina's poetry and visual art dance across the pages as a pas-de-deux opening with Pnina age ten through a period of quiet contemplation and connection before culminating in a beautiful and touching tribute to her late husband Edmond Granirer (Eddy). This poignant collection serves as an important reminder of the tenuous nature of our own existence, the incredible power of art, love and community, and the awe-inspiring mystery, beauty and hope we can all find when we take the time to reconnect with nature and ourselves.

— Paul F. Crawford
Director/Curator
Penticton Art Gallery

"I speak with paint and brush" writes the author of this beautiful collection. Granirer's intermingling of poetry and visual art gives us a profound glimpse into two visions. In one, we see the mysterious yet inanimate stones in the painting. In another, with the buoyant sea ever present, the stones come alive through words. "I sit alone and listen to the whispering of stones," she writes. About the sea, she speaks of how "Giants' hands pull back the waves." She doesn't shout but almost whispers the powerful themes of war, plague, sadness, joy and memory, questioning the human condition with delicacy and compassion.

— Lillian Boraks-Nemetz
author of *Out of the Dark* and *Mouth of Truth: Buried Secrets*

This collection of poems encompasses a range of subject matters, offering personal reflections that are variously joyous, sharp and heartbreaking. Interspersed with Granirer's writing are artworks spanning many years of painting. Time collapses within these pages. They offer a window into a vivid life lived in extraordinary times, and a woman enchanted with the world around her.

— George Harris
Director/Curator
Two Rivers Gallery, Prince George, BC

Artist Pnina Granirer is also a poet who has written verse since 1945, when the 10-year-old expressed her joy at the end of WW2. The poems range in space from Romania to Israel to Canada, and include many vignettes recorded with a painter's eye and a haiku-like intensity. Some are vividly illustrated with images selected from her long career in visual art. Among my favourites were descriptions of a racoon washing its paws, a glass of sangria in Spain, and eroded sandstones rocks in the Gulf Islands. The book ends with a moving elegy for her recently deceased husband. Readers will find much to treasure in this rich selection from the work of a talented poet-painter.

— Graham Good
Professor Emeritus of English at UBC
translator of *Rilke's Late Poetry* and *Goethe's Poems*

BOOKS BY AND ABOUT PNINA GRANIRER

Pnina Granirer, Portrait Of An Artist by Ted Lindberg

The Trials Of Eve, limited edition, Alcuin Citation Award, and softcover edition

Light Within The Shadows: A Painter's Memoir

Garden of Words

Garden of Words

Pnina Granirer

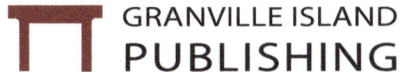
GRANVILLE ISLAND PUBLISHING

Copyright © 2022 Pnina Granirer

All rights reserved. No part of this publication may be reproduced, stored in a retrieval system or transmitted, in any form or by any means, without prior permission of the publisher or, in the case of photocopying or other reprographic copying, a license from Access Copyright, the Canadian Copyright Licensing Agency, www.accesscopyright.ca, 1-800-893-5777, info@accesscopyright.ca. Due to the dynamic nature of the internet, website addresses and contents may have changed since publication.

ISBN: 978-1-989467-59-6 (paperback)
ISBN: 978-1-989467-58-9 (ebook)

Editor: Kyle Hawke
Book designer: Omar Gallegos
Art Photographer: Janet Lee

Granville Island Publishing Ltd.
105 – 1496 Cartwright St.
#14354, Granville Island
Vancouver, BC, Canada, V6H 4J6

604-688-0320 / 1-877-688-0320
info@granvilleislandpublishing.com
www.granvilleislandpublishing.com

for Eddy, my beloved life companion

"Painting is poetry which is seen and not heard,
and poetry is a painting which is heard but not seen."

— *Leonardo da Vinci*
as cited by *Francesco Melzi*
in *The Paragone* from *A Treatise on Painting (1651)*

Contents

Preface	ix
May 9, 1945	x
Garden of Words	xii
Sea and Stones	1
Pandemic	31
Dancers	47
Memories of Spain	57
This and That	71
Closure	97

Preface

Unexpected and unplanned, like small gifts offered by a kind friend, poems have been forming in my head ever since I was a child. For no reason at all, events, places and thoughts have compelled me to put pen to paper. There were long pauses, weeks, months and years, when the poems were absent, and then—my hand would scribble words on paper again.

A small book with frayed blue covers sitting quietly on my shelf bears witness to poems written from the age of 9 to 12, in Romanian. One poem expresses the joy and happiness of a 9-year-old when on August 23, 1944, the Soviet Red Army entered our town as the cattle cars were waiting at the train station to take us away to the concentration camps. It had been a narrow escape, indeed! But on May 9, 1945, it was finally over for everyone.

I believe that the poem on the following page would serve well as the first words for this book.

May 9, 1945

• Translation of a poem written in Romania by the author at age 10

After five years of horror, suffering and barbary
We may live in brotherhood at last!
These were five years of never-ending horror
The Germans passing all through sword and fire.

But this time is gone for good!
The wailing has now ended
Russians, British and Americans, without much ado,
Chased the Nazis home and beat them through and through.

May 9! You are the day of our salvation
And long-awaited day of happiness!
May 9! You erase all sighing
And bring us beautiful blue skies.
The one man who could not enjoy your gift

And disappeared on gossamer wings
Is Franklin Delano Roosevelt, the always smiling friend
of children and all people.
The world weeps for him and will weep forever.
With bitter tears, tears of blood.

In wailing of sirens and light of fireworks
The longed-for day of peace arrived.
And now, when fighting is at last all over
And everyone feels happiness again
Let's wish to all of us in joy and laughter:
"May God preserve the peace forever after!"

Paula Solomon (now Pnina Granirer)
4th elementary grade
Institute Sancta Maria

Garden of Words

I am a painter

I speak with paint and brush
my words are written
with colour and with line.
My stories
are told
in images
and shapes
    to be deciphered

    like ancient hieroglyphs.
Yet —
words
are instruments of power
woven threads of sound
    binding the loose pages of our lives.

By speaking, godlike
one may conjure
a Universe.

I should so like to plant
a garden of words
in my field of colours

and watch them grow.

Sea and Stones

Eternity

The meaning of eternity
lies at my feet.

Washed by waves
this carved rock
has waited eons
to be discovered.

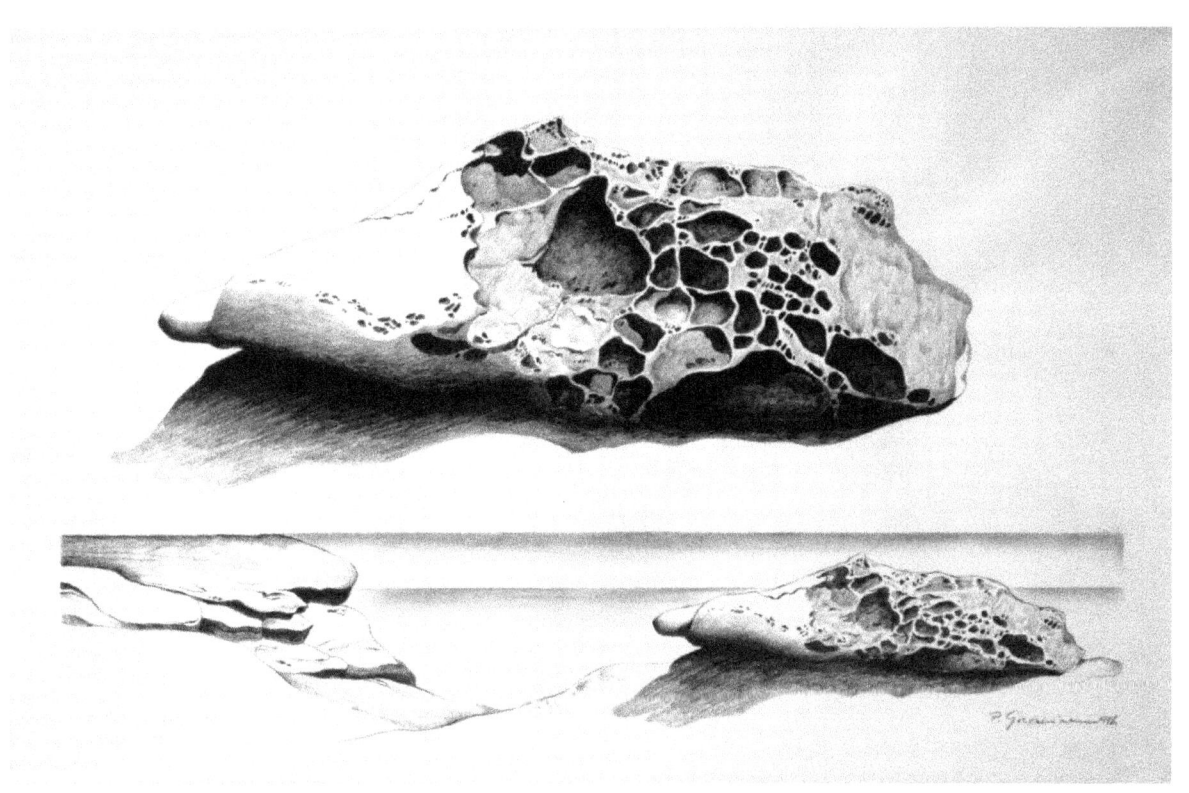

Stone, 1986, graphite and coloured pencil on paper, 22×30 in.

The Game

Last evening
I watched waves
pulled by the sliver
of a slender new moon
    conquer the beach.

With roaring sound
the hungry sea devoured the naked rocks
a game in which
there was one winner only.

Then — it was over.
The stones had vanished
beneath the watery expanse.

Next morning
the sea reluctantly retreated
and whispered like a faithful lover:
I shall be back tonight
We'll play this game again.

Big City

In the big city
    I am lulled to sleep
      by the hum of cars whizzing by.

On the seashore
    I am kept awake
by the rhythmic sound of crushing waves.

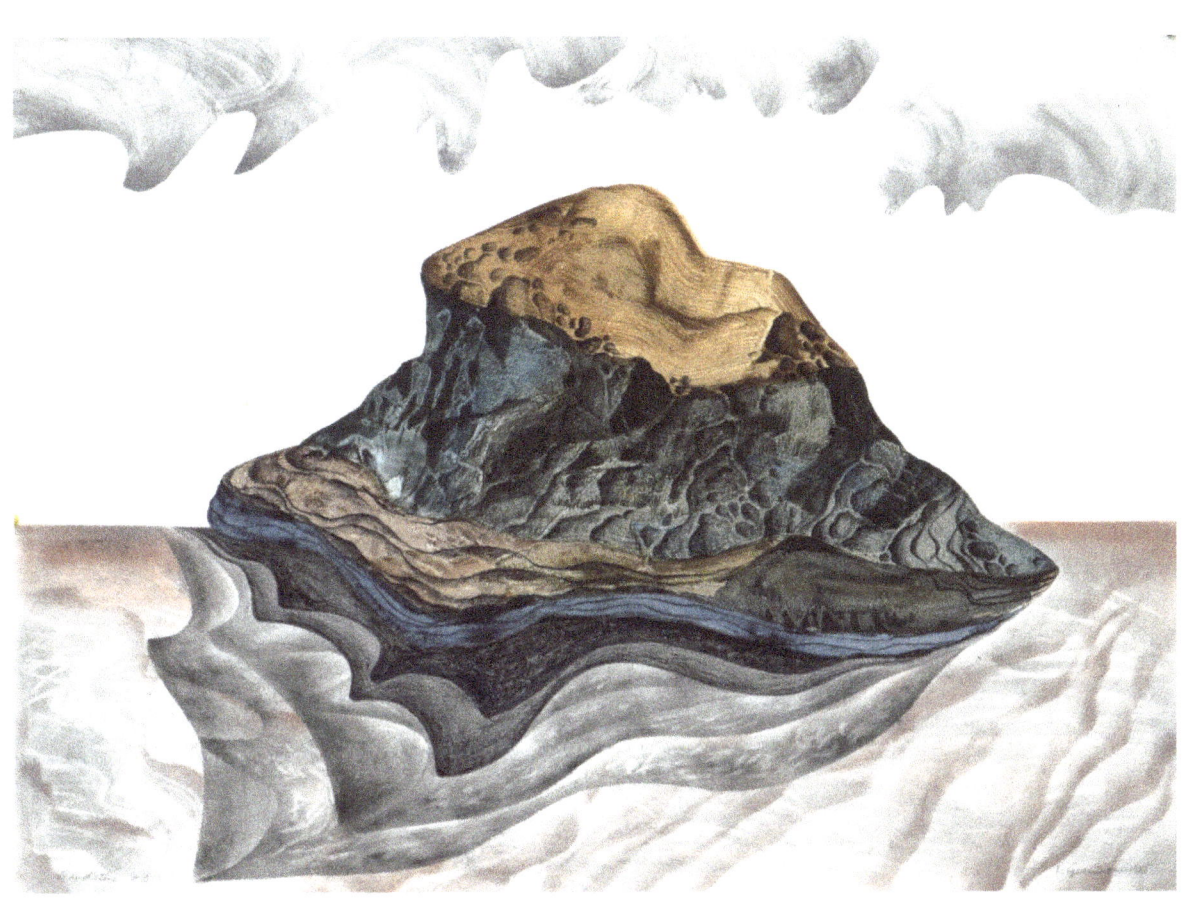

Sandstone 3, 1985, mixed media on paper, 22×30 in.

Lesson of the Sea

Polished stones
smooth eggs
of soft greys and fleshy pinks
nurtured by the waves
never to hatch.
There is no button one may push
to stop the never ceasing sound

of water crashing on the shore.
No computer one can program
to silence it
even for a second.

The sea laughs and sings
    as it teaches us a lesson
        about infinity.

Beach

The tide is out
the air is still.
Prehistoric monsters turned to stone
are baking in the burning sun

a herd surprised in flight
frozen in time.

Black shadows
hide
in dark, smooth holes
carved deeply in the rocky flesh.

I walk upon the backs of silent creatures
transformed
by an invisible magician.

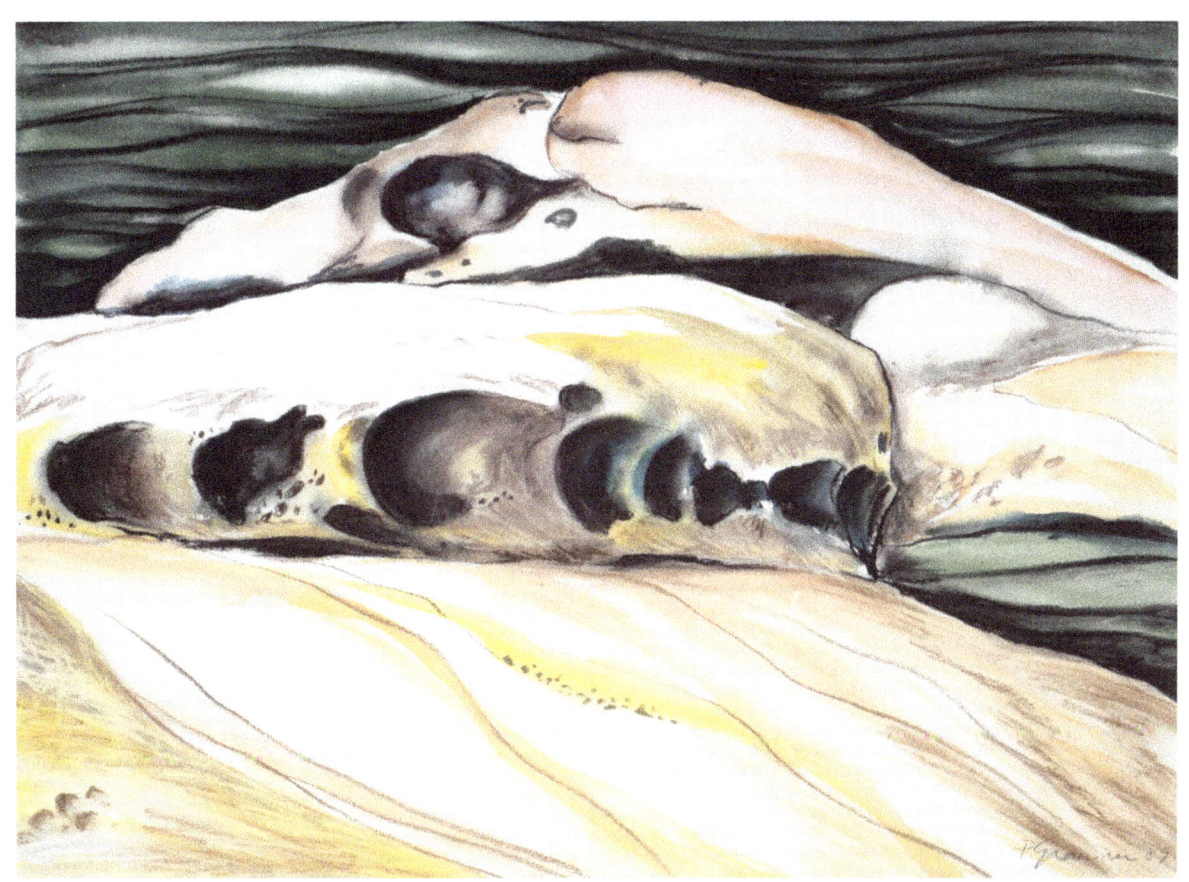

Formation, 1989, mixed media on paper, 22×30 in.

Lust Amid the Barnacles

Small rocks strewn on sandy shore
    glisten with sparks of silver chips

lumps of stone
shaped into exquisite gem-like sculptures
reflect the rays of midday sun

*A couple of shiny green flies
buzz lustily amid the barnacles,
intent on making love.*

Midmorning Sun

Midmorning sun
mantle of white, hot light.
The air is still as dry paint on a canvas.

Eerie sight of stones
     becoming bones
shapes fit for dreams.

Sleeping beauties whose prince will never come.

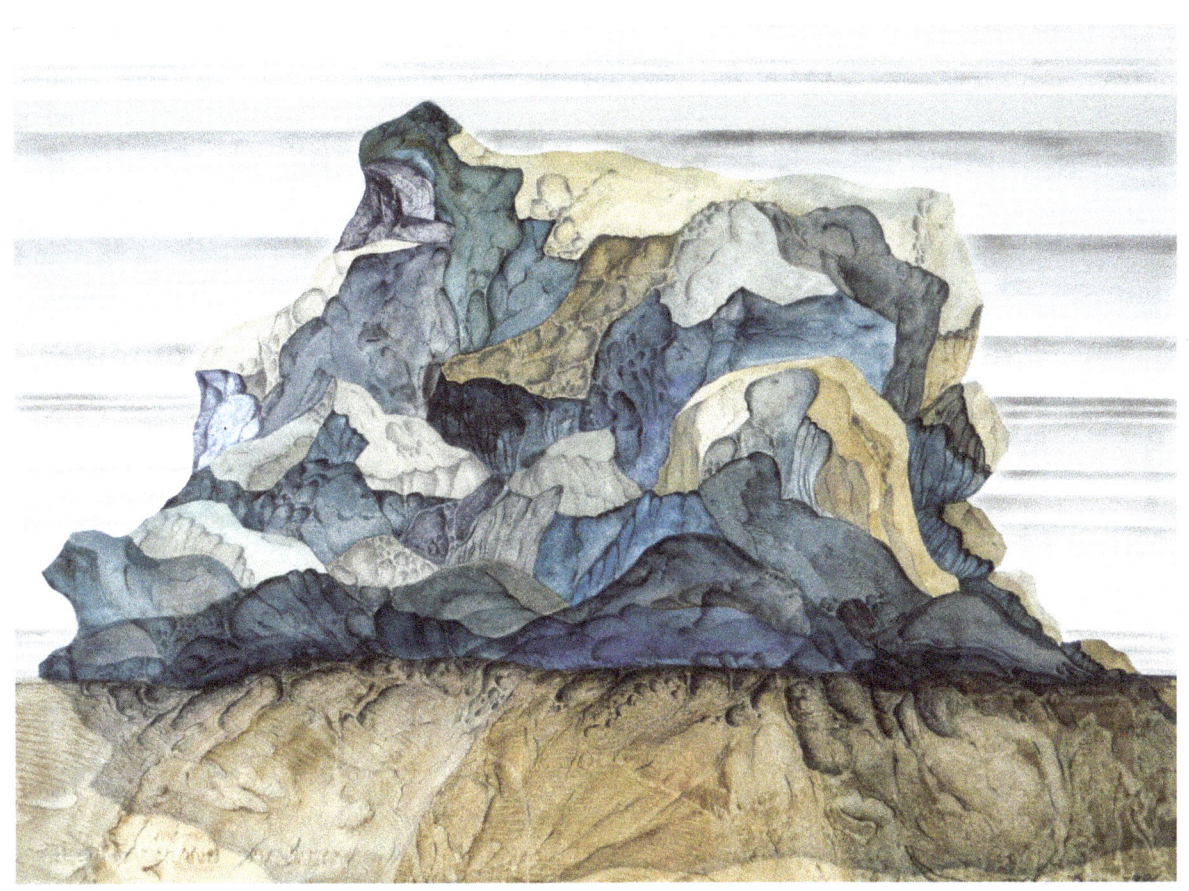

Sandstone #5, 1981, mixed media on paper, 22×30 in.

These Shores

I love these stones

these silent carvings
sculpted
in a relentless, patient, everlasting game
by multitudes of microscopic grains
of salt and sand and wind.

*Geologists have all the answers
            of 'how' and 'why'
But I, in speechless wonder
Shall bow my head in silence
and worship them
with pen and paint and brush.*

Question

How many before me
    sat on this rock,
    this loyal, silent lover
    of a moody ocean?

A bridal veil of frothy lace
hides its glistening seaweed hair.
It covers it noisily

    then slips off
    only to return
    in a perpetuum mobile.

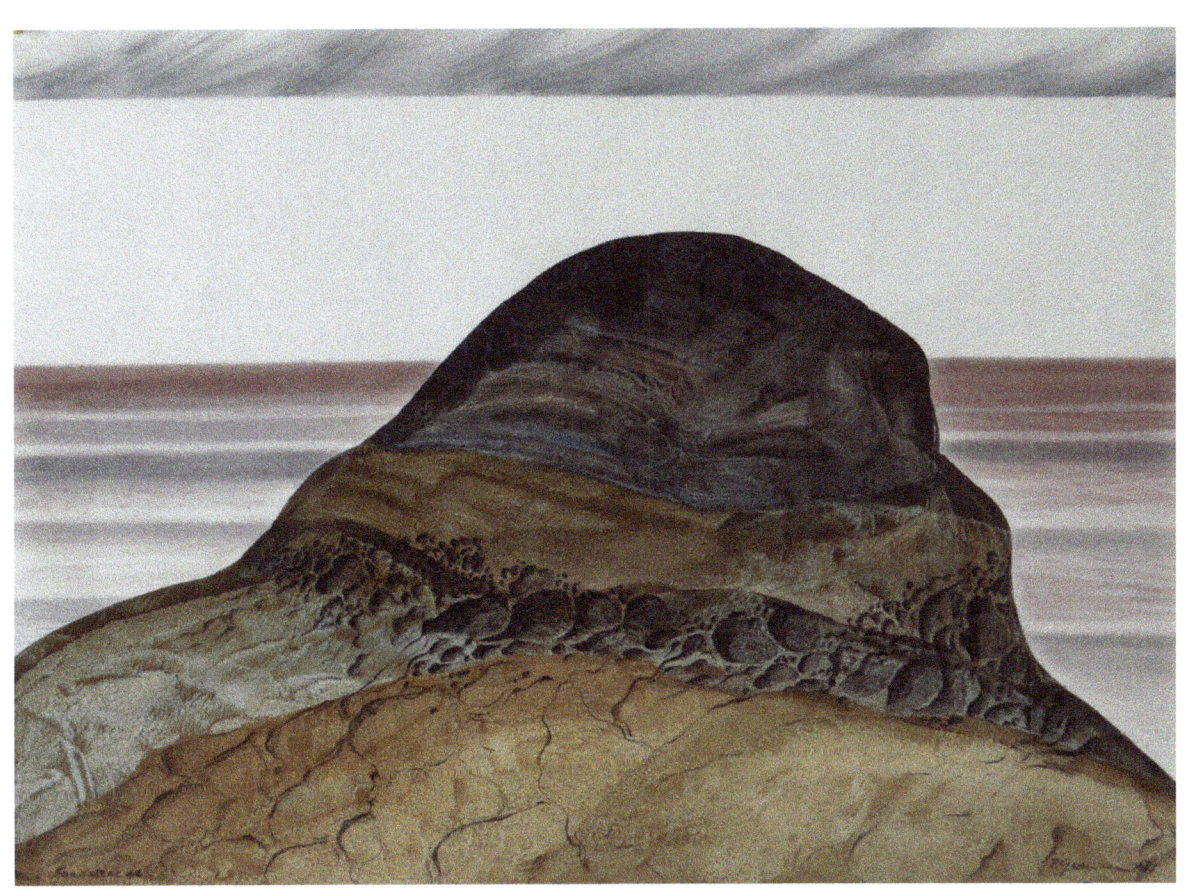

Sandstone #2, 1985, mixed media on paper, 22×30 in.

Sea and Stones

Vision

What is the flashing light
of inspiration
the unexpected spark, the new idea, the vision
or the revelation
that penetrates the artists mind?

Stones washed by waves on a deserted beach
immobile, silent, deeply carved
spoke to me one day in summer.

Enthralled by their strength and beauty
I made them mine forever
on canvas and on paper.

Sea and Stones

The Whispering of Stones

"Haunting", they call my paintings.
These tortured lumps of rock
are deemed disturbing
like bones of long-dead monsters
rotting in the sun.

I sit alone
and listen
to the quiet whispering of stones.

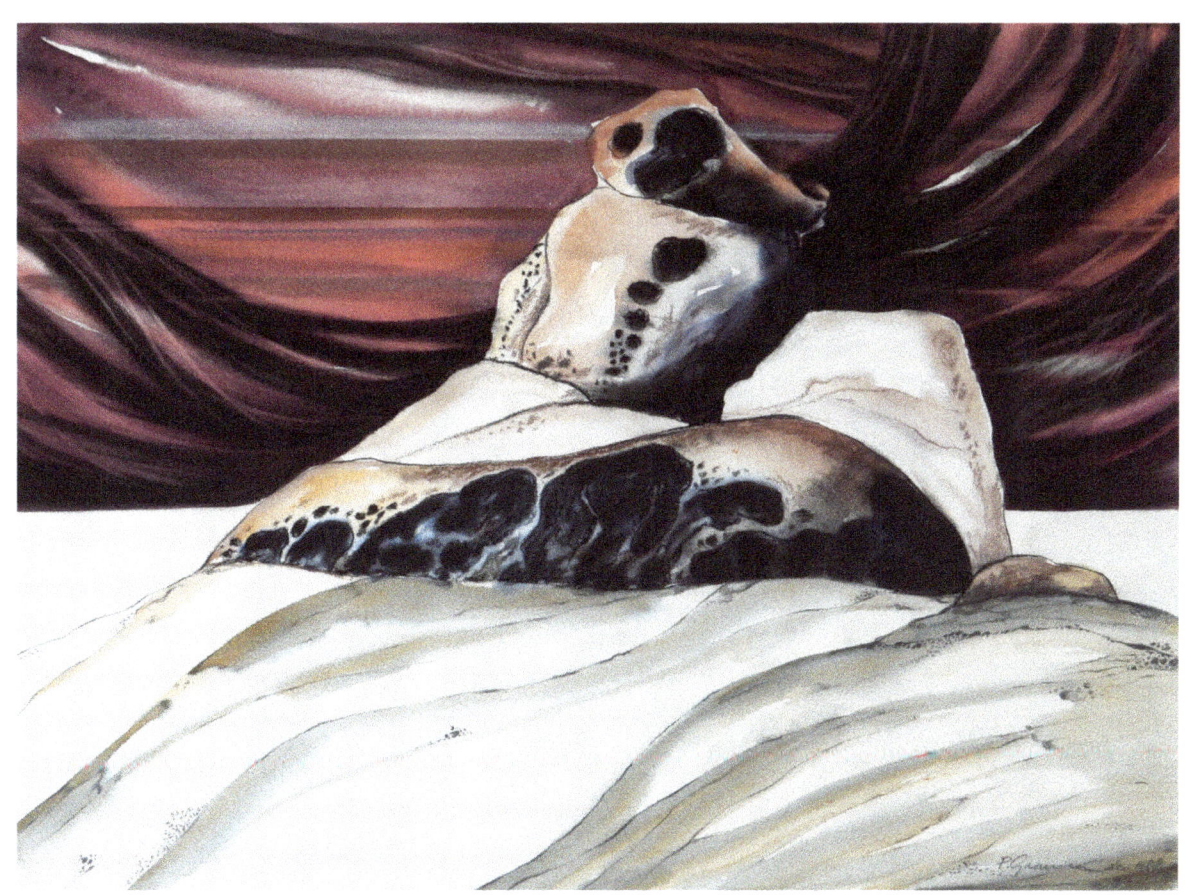

Centre Stage, 1988, mixed media on paper, 22×30 in.

Song to the Sea

There is not much new to say
              about the sea
enough has been written
to cover it with paper from shore to shore.

And yet
Listening to the pounding of the waves
 I am afraid of its strength.

To a Rock

You are a lifeless thing
they say
"Inanimate" they call you.

And yet
    encoded in your depth
    you hold
        the secrets of the earth.

If you could talk
we would laugh together

remembering.

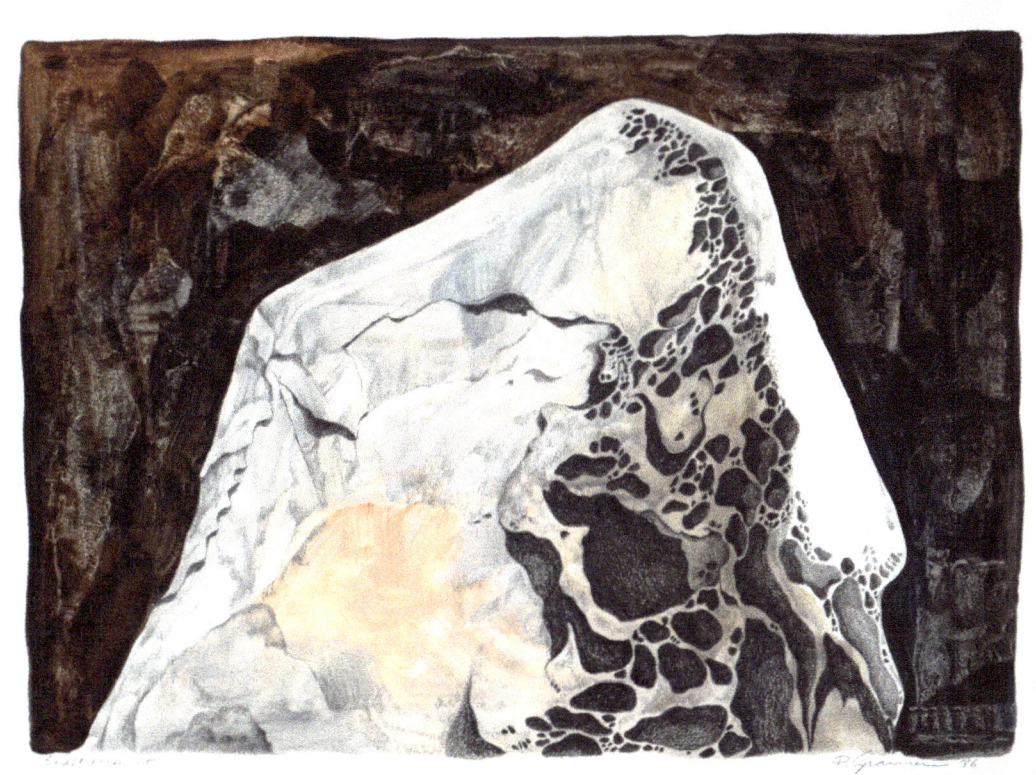

Small Monument, 1987, mixed media on paper, 15×19 in.

Waves

Giants' hands
   pull back the waves.

Later
the morning sun
dries the pebbles on the beach
such as a housewife
who does not like
         a wet floor in her parlour.

Pandemic 2

Plague

Seen only through microscopes in busy labs
pretty balls
float in the air
sharp tentacles
inject their poison on unsuspecting victims.

The sun still shines
trees sway in gentle breeze
daffodils and tulips, spring flowers
bloom in my garden.

Birds fly and fill the air with song
ants hurry on their path
and weeds spread on the lawn.

All is well outside my garden — or so it seems.
On vacant streets
abandoned stores closed tight
an empty set
waiting for actors to appear.

All Together Now

This novel enemy is democratic.

In its indifference
all prey is equal.

Bribes cannot appease it

and no exalted rank
will make it spare its victims.

There are no privileged exemptions.

Covid-19 is basking in its fame
the media is trumpeting its name
Corona　　Corona　　Corona

We're all together now.

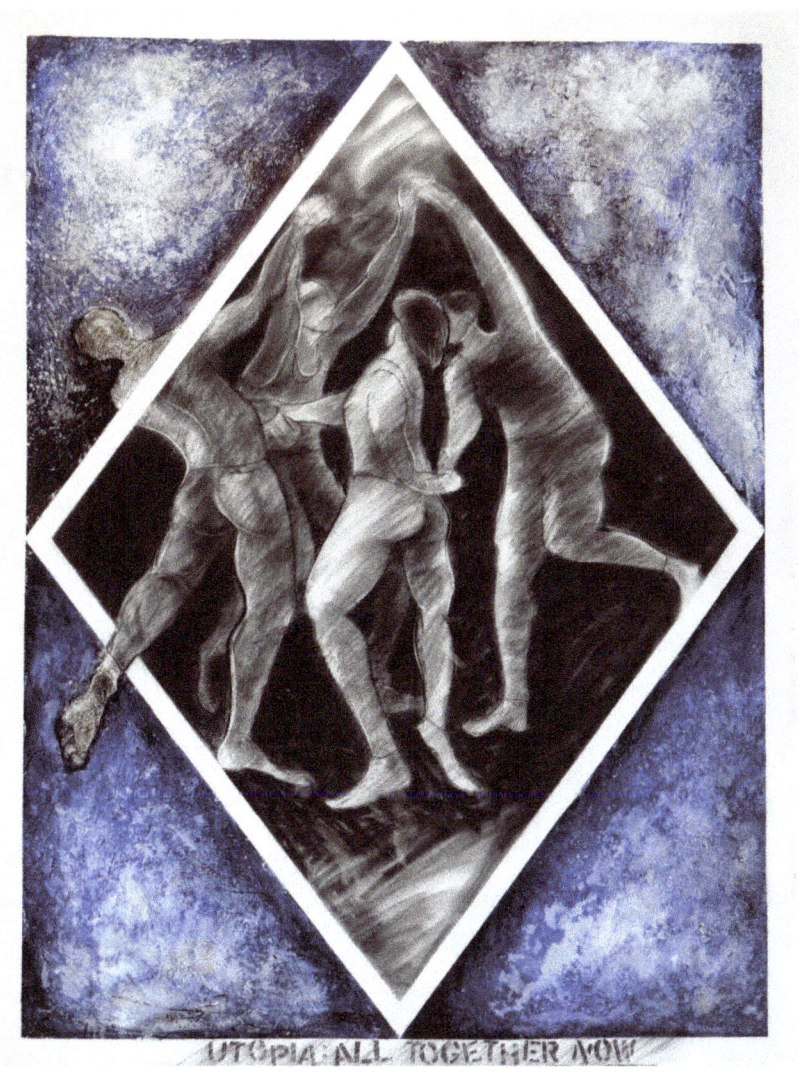

Utopia — All Together Now, 2008, mixed media on canvas, 48×36 in.

A Ray of Light

A war is on.
No armies, nor powerful dictators —
this enemy
      invisible and unforgiving
      invades the earth.

I close my eyes and shut my ears
I need to know that life goes on
that this pandemic
will soon be gone.

I need to know
that people love and smile
and smell the perfume of flowers blooming in the garden.

. . . .

A ray of light shines in the darkness
kind friends have left food at my door.

Perfection

The evening sun
gently warms my back.
Low over the city
white clouds, like decorations on a cake
hang still and solemn.
The perfume of a lilac tree
    fills the air.

Across the waters of the inlet
Grouse Mountain looms
snow sparkling like a crown.

Dancing together
    two birds flash by
    and quickly disappear.

I hear the hum of traffic up the hill.
A perfect day.

The mask, my shield against Corona
    is waiting on the table.

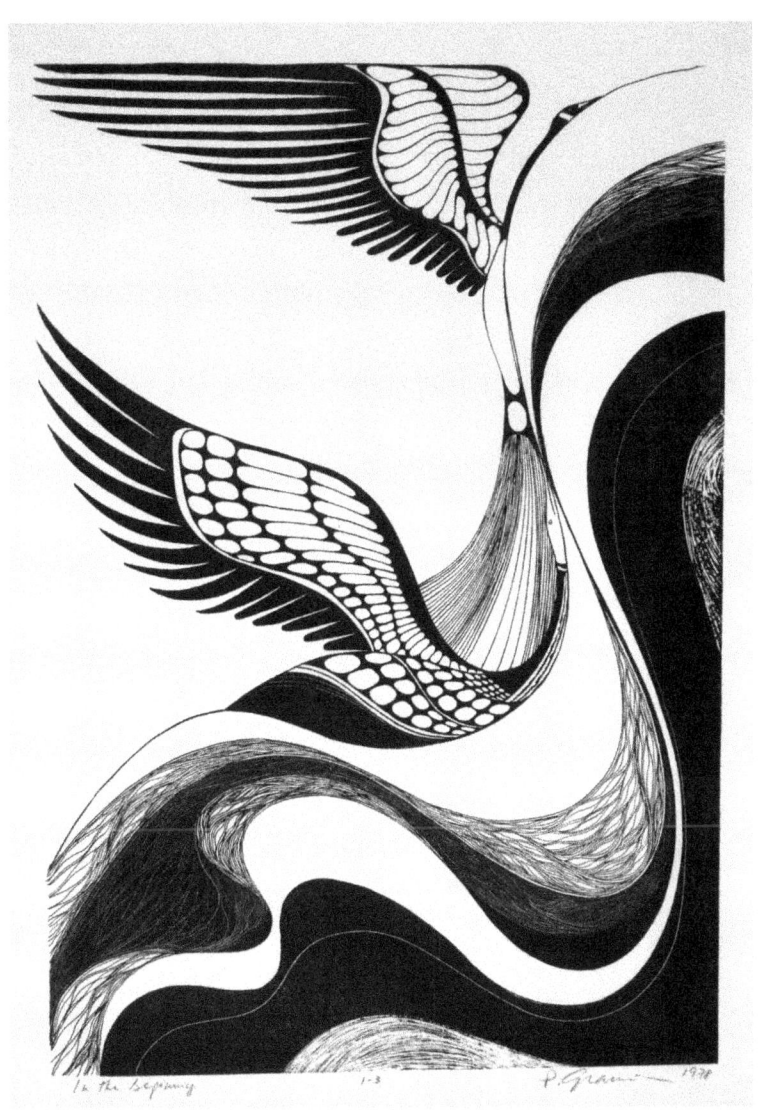

In the beginning, 1978, lithograph, 14×11 in.

Raccoon

For Phyllis

A friend drops by to say hello
to wish me
Happy Mother's Day.
We stand apart and chat
by the small pond in my garden.
No visiting up close, no hugs;
    a virus now controls our lives
    and social distance is the law.

Among the flowers by the pond
a gentle stir
catches our eye.
An unexpected visitor
is here.

A large raccoon
attempts to reach the water.
He walks around, from right to left
oblivious to the observing eyes
who watch this rare performance
with bated breath.

At last success!
He finds the spot.
We see him wash his tiny paws
    and hear the water splashing.

He surely knows the rules
how to avoid
Covid-19.

Stillness

The sky is blue again
    the smog left China's crowded cities
    and people breathe clean air.

Empty streets, few cars and no planes spewing fumes.

New words appear:
    masks and social distance
    quarantine and isolation.
We wash our hands with much more care than ever.

This novel tyrant
    more powerful than any despot
    has changed the world.

It seems that time has stopped.
    Friends and family are images on screens
    Zoom is the new king.

It is unknown
how long the fear will last.

All is still.

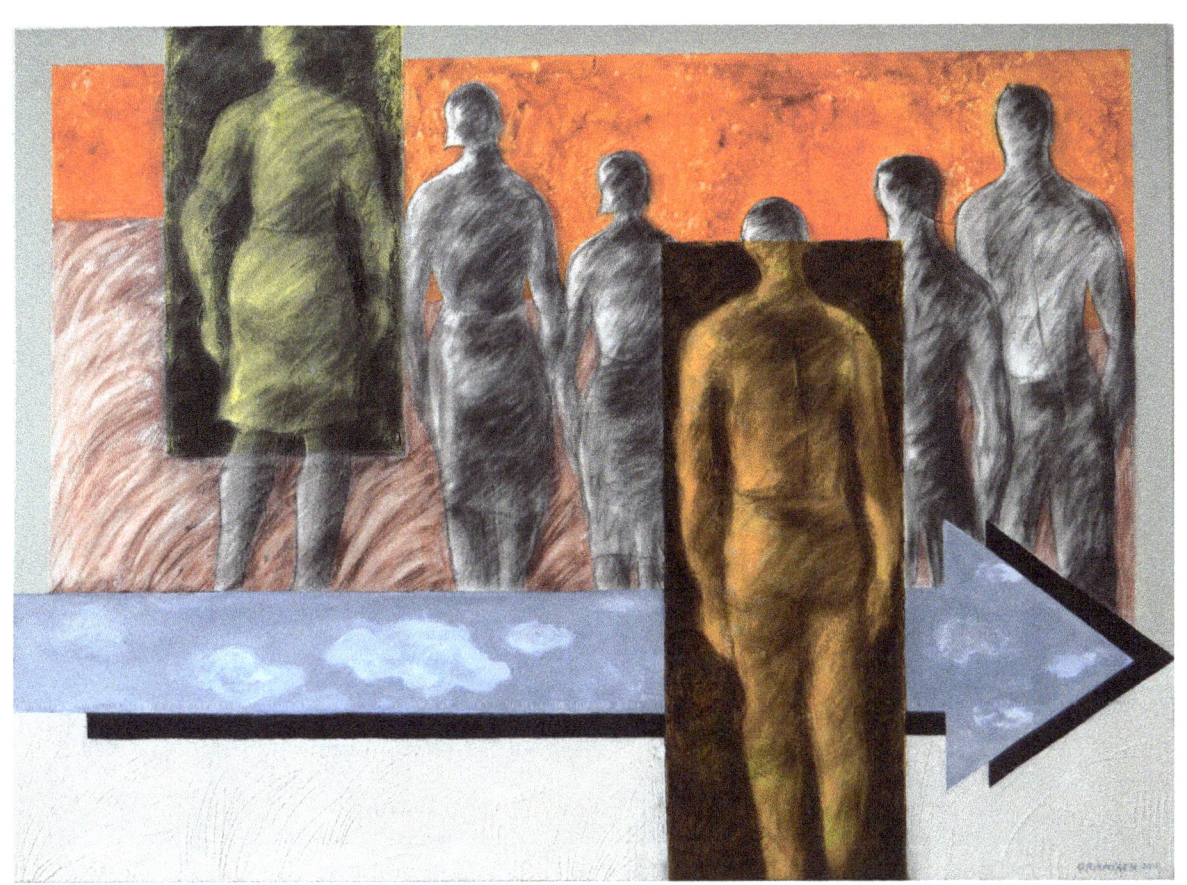

Stillness, 2011, mixed media on canvas, 36×48 in.

Reminder

*From time to time
and without warning
great plagues engulf the earth.*

*Guns and mighty armies
cannot defend us
all we can do is*

hide
            hide
                        hide.
Powerless gods
stare blankly in the empty churches

helpless and deaf to prayers.

Dancers 3

Dancer

On the dark stage
a brilliant beam of light reveals a human figure.

The dancer's body
weightless and free
defies the strong pull of the earth.
His graceful movements belie
the long and arduous hours
of bone-breaking work.

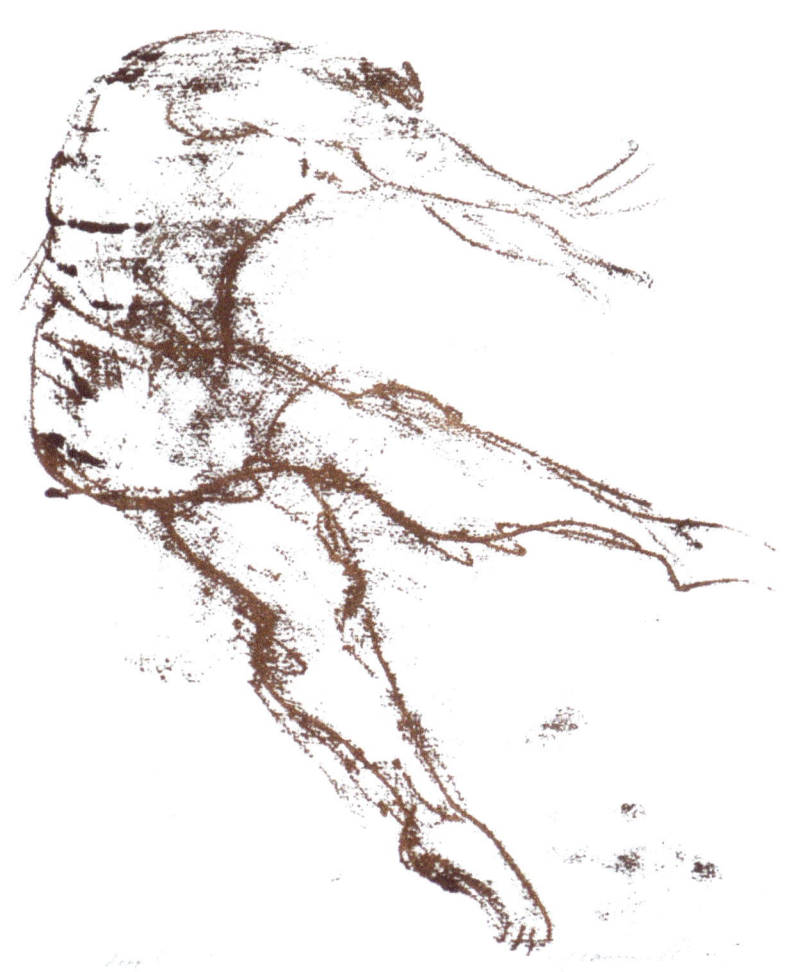

Leap, 2002, monoprint on paper, 22×15 in.

Performance

Swept by the music
bodies leap and bend.
Arms rise in supplication
embracing, touching
    breaking free.
Bodies are lifted to unexpected heights
then land as light as feathers.

What is the urge that drives
these graceful dancers
to challenge
      the strong pull of the earth?

I need to capture
the beauty, the daring and the freedom
of these young bodies
and make them live forever in my
paintings.

Stop the Time

Cori leads
 my drawings follow.

I try to stop the time
treasure this moment
and put it down on paper
 where it will last forever.

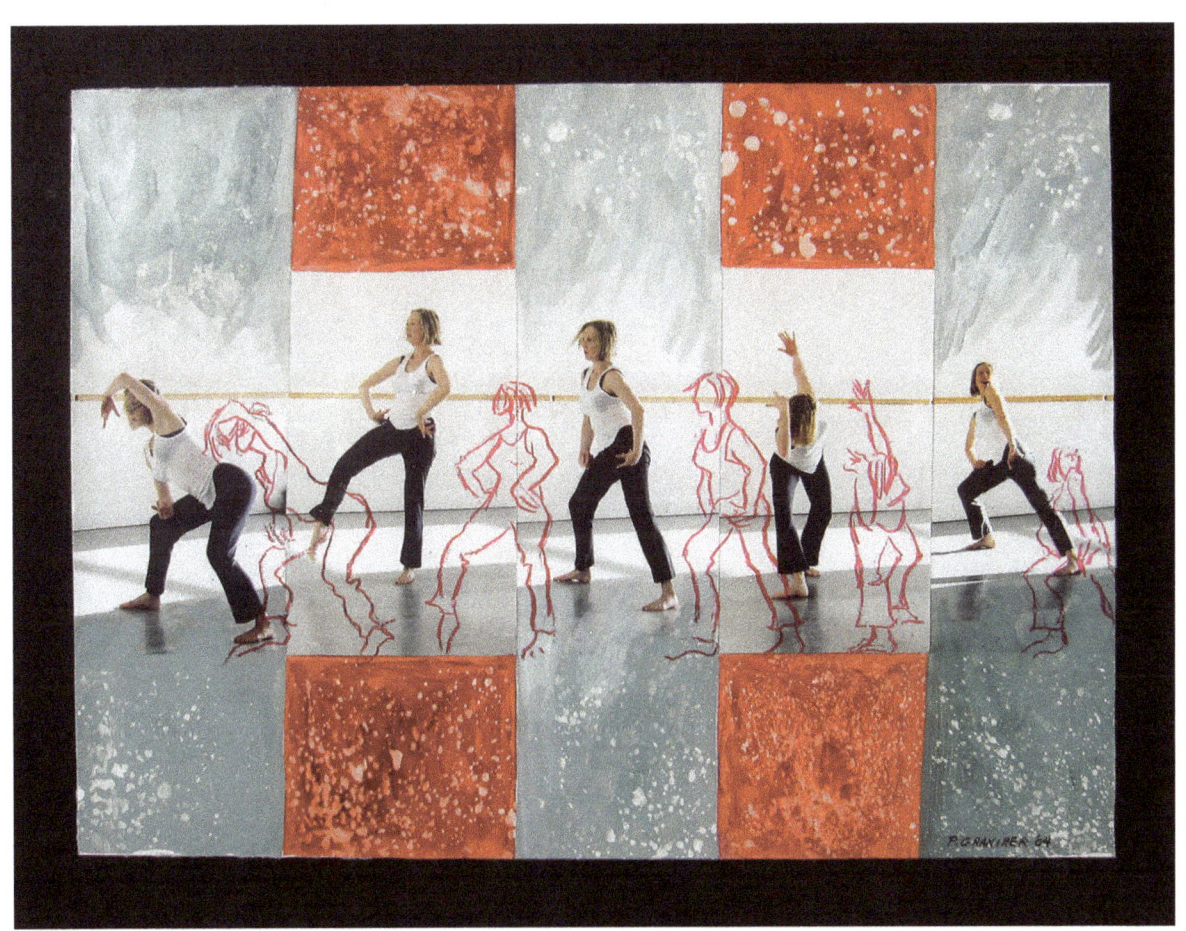

Cori's Dance, 2003, mixed media on paper and mylar, 14×20 in.

To My Friend, Cori

On a large sheet of transparent mylar
a figure comes to life
with quick strokes of my brush.

Raising her arm
she floats in space
frozen in time.

Unlike my drawing that is fated
    to raise her arm forever,

Cori's living movement is brief
like the flitting
      of a butterfly's wing,
a prelude
to graceful steps that follow
captured
not by my brush
but by the clicks of cameras

          and then they're gone.

Memories of Spain

Castles in Spain

Towers and stone walls perch haughtily on Andalusian heights

skeletons of history
exclamation marks left behind
by long-gone rulers.

Among these ruins
the wind still whispers tales
     of war and bloodshed
     in the name of Allah
     and auto-da-fés for Jesus Christ.

Down in the green valley
silent in the blazing sun,
the Roman ramparts, the mosque now turned cathedral,
still stand
beside a village white as snow.

How did these people live and love
and fight and die
and pray and sing
and work and eat
and plant their vines

beneath the towers of this alcàzar,
this fortress on the hill?

Toledo

On the terrace of the parador
we drink sangria from elegant, tall glasses
and savour the juicy orange slices
drowning in the ruby-tinted wine.
    The soft evening sun
      covers the city across the valley
    in a net of golden thread.

Wedding guests wander about
like actors in search of a play.
The women, in party gowns and flowers in their hair
converse with knowing smiles.
The men, handsome and stiff in their formal suits
sweat secretly in the summer heat.

At our feet
Toledo.
A giant canvas stretched below translucent skies
hovers between reality and the vision of a great
painter.
Around its waist, the Tajo river glitters
like a silver ribbon
tied to a birthday gift.

Enchanted moments on this hill
as we gaze down on history.

I shall always remember my birthday in Toledo
on the terrace of the parador,
the glistening sangria
waiting in the cool wine glasses.

Visit with El Greco

Today I shall visit
Domenico Theotocopoulos the Greek.

No need to call
    for an appointment
No need to check
    if he is home
No need to ring the bell
and wait for footsteps
    coming to the door
or to apologize that
I am 400 years late.

At the entrance of the modest house
tourists wait, clutching their tickets,
curious and eager to discover
the secrets of this man, this painter
who delved deep into the human soul
and found immortality.

I feel like an intruder
in someone's private bedroom.

Stones Are Forever

Grey stones
white stones
red and ochre.

Dressed stones
carved stones
smooth or broken.

Peaks of mountains
castle walls
fortress ramparts.

Stones are forever, thought
a power-thirsty king
and built himself a castle on a hill.

It is still there,
looking down at the olive groves
and the green fields of Andalucia.

The king is just a memory
                      long gone.

Granada

It is very hot in Granada on the afternoon of the Semana Santa, the Holy Week. The old part of town beckons and we walk its winding streets, admiring its ornate buildings, the wrought-iron balconies with their intricate designs and the carvings on the stone walls.

Suddenly, with no warning, the empty streets are filled with people and the sound of beating drums. Men emerge in two single-file rows, walking slowly in the middle of the narrow street, wearing white pointed hoods with thin slits for the eyes, while holding long, red candles in their hands. Their purple robes are tied with ropes around the waist; they walk leisurely, in step with the ominous sound of the drums. Some of them hold large crosses. One of the leaders carries a crown of thorns on a crimson velvet pillow.

They are drawing close now, so close that I can see their eyes gleaming through the slits, as they advance towards me.

My stomach tightens with fear. I feel as I had been thrown five hundred years back, standing on a street in Catholic Spain; the Inquisition is here. I am a Jew and it is coming for me. I am a Muslim and I am afraid. I am a black woman and here is the KKK coming. I am terrified. The sight of those pointed hoods unleashes a flood of emotion I did not know I was capable of. My anxiety is close to panic.

The sinister figures stop very near to me. I hear their muffled voices under their cowls making small talk, laughing. Small children approach fearlessly, gathering drippings from the candles in plastic bags. Why? For souvenirs? Good luck? There are real people inside these clothes, people who live in this neighbourhood, whose friends have come to join the procession and savour the sight.

I ask a bystander what all this signifies and I realize that the crowds are blissfully unaware of the history hiding behind these hoods, these robes and these candles. "They are penitents," I am told. "They cover their faces so as not to show their 'pain' at the death of Jesus, our Saviour."

Five hundred years after the Inquisition, the burnings and auto-da-fés are pushed out of memory, conveniently forgotten, but the ceremonies persist; the dark past is not taught in Spanish schools. It has been turned into an Easter celebration, a parade, a fun event.

At the end of the long procession comes the 'pièce de résistance': the ornate float carrying the statue of the Virgin. It is massive. The huge cart is carried on the shoulders of sixty men hidden from view by a red velvet curtain, who train for months for the honour of carrying the Madonna. One can see only their feet, wearing running shoes, shuffling in unison at the beat of the drums.

The statue of the Holy Virgin is an imposing sight. She is dressed in rich robes of silk, velvet and brocade, embroidered with gold thread in intricate patterns, adorned with real jewels. Leaning slightly forward, her arms raised in benediction, her long train floating behind, the Madonna is marching, swaying rhythmically in step with the carriers below. Protected by a red velvet canopy, she is surrounded by flowers and burning candles—a regal sight and a feast for the eyes. The Goddess is back, worshipped and adored as in the days of old. As the French, who are so good at finding 'le mot juste', would say: plus ça change, plus c'est la même chose. Does it matter if her name is Isis, looking for her son, Horus? Or perhaps Ishtar, Queen of Heaven, or Juno, Queen of the Gods? The age-old ritual of Goddess worship is clearly practiced here, in this very Catholic procession, in this most Catholic city of Seville.

Witnessing this event rich in pageantry and colour with its sinister overtones, one cannot but think that the pagan religions have won, after all. Like strong viruses, they have adapted to the antibiotics of monotheism and appear now in such perfect disguise that one is not even aware of their presence. Perhaps the human species needs to understand the Universe and make sense of the mystery by seeing and touching the gods, assigning them control over good and evil and worshipping them as powerful idols.

It is almost dark. A crowd of followers trails the procession back to the church, the permanent home of this elegant Madonna, where the ceremonies will continue until late into the night. This is the celebration of the 'Reconquista', the victory of the Catholic kings who took Granada back from the Muslims—the victory of the Cross and the defeat of the Crescent.

But the true, hidden victory belongs to the pagan Goddess.

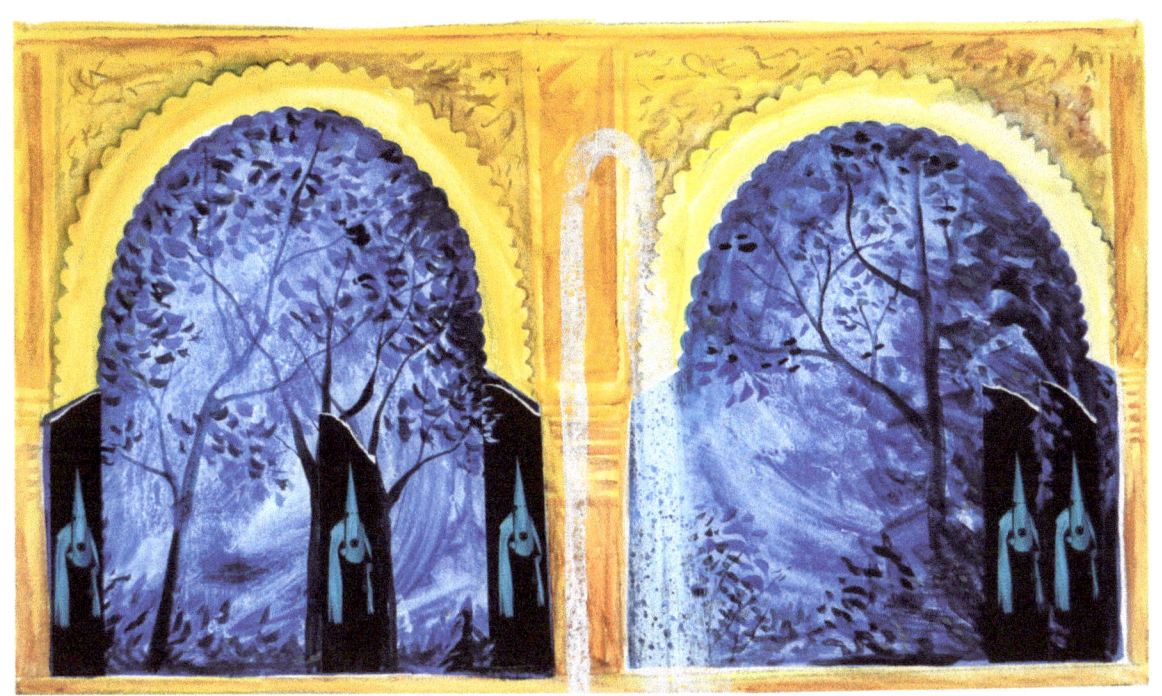

Windows (detail), 1997, mixed media on paper, full size 40×30 in.

This and That

Incantation for a Magic Circle

The wind is howling through the branches
man is killing man somewhere
each one of us lives in a circle
    we just don't know it's there.

I hide my head under my pillow
when thunder shakes my bed at night
I'll step into the perfect circle
and will be safe inside.

No evil will befall me
the devil cannot reach me
the circle will enclose me
safe forever.

The clouds, they race above me
deep forests do embrace me
a seagull calls me, calls me
I shall be coming.

When waves do crash around me
and darkness does enclose me
the circle will protect me
    safe forever.

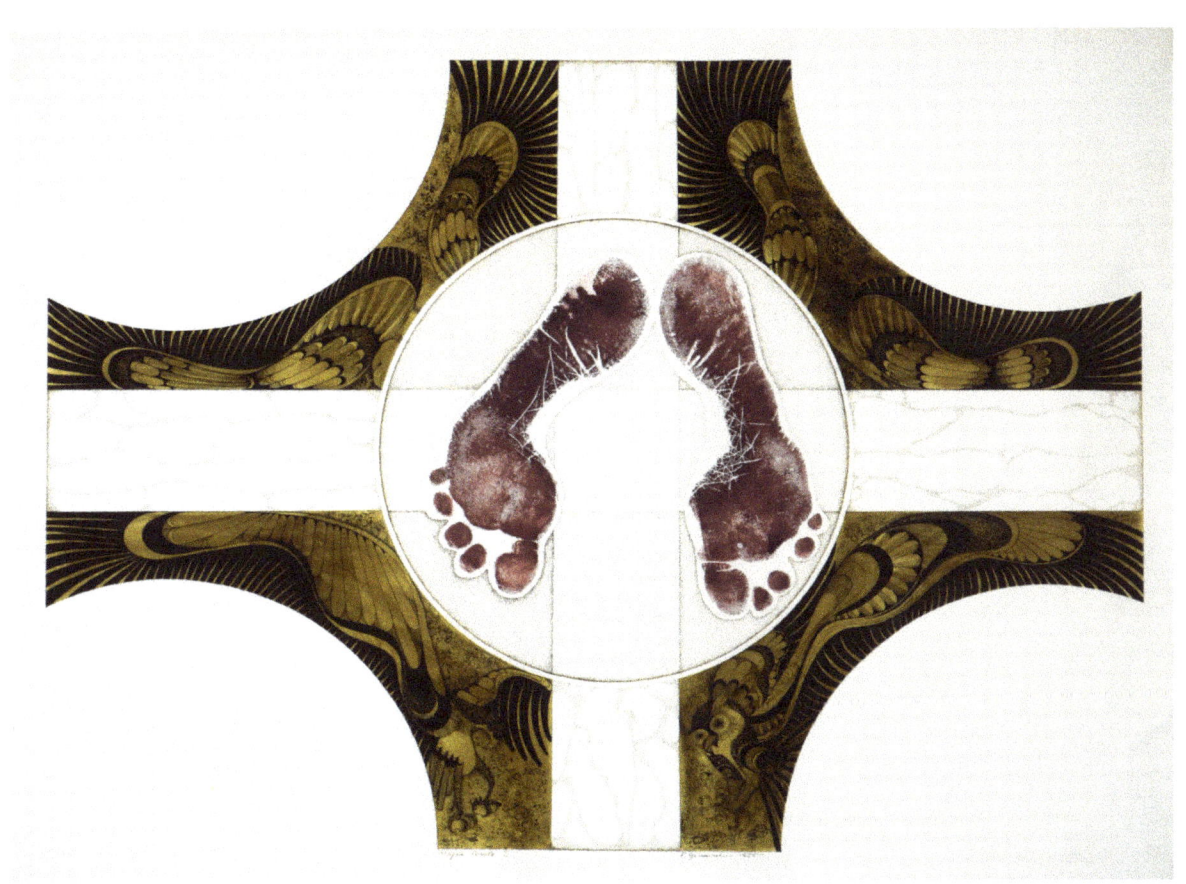
Magic Circle, 1975, mixed media on paper, 22×30 in.

Soul

So much
has been said and written
about the soul.

It can't be touched
    and yet it hurts
it can't be seen
    yet it rejoices
it can't be heard
    and yet it speaks
it has no shape
    and yet it rules.

Tell me, I beg you:
how does one heal
    a wounded soul?

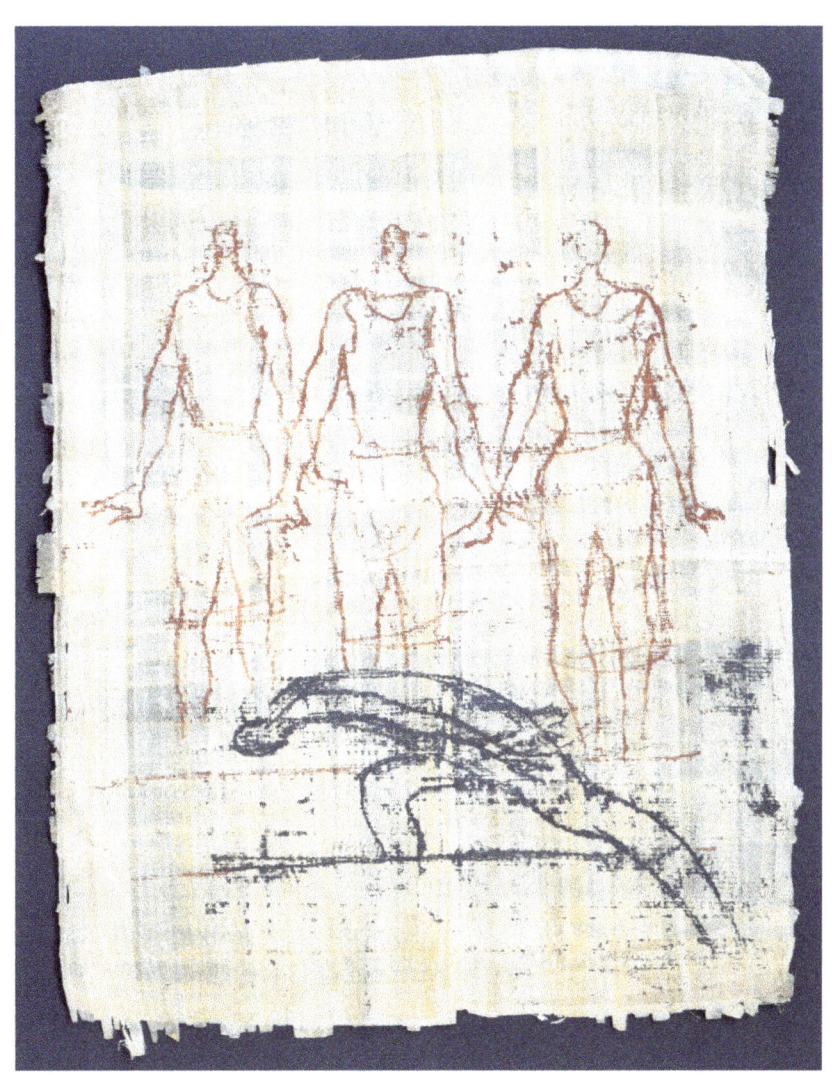

Who Am I?, 2006, monoprint on papyrus, 19×14 in.

City Woman

"When I look at a mountain
what is there to do? I mean, what can one really do with it?"
she asks.
"At least, while lying on the beach
I get a tan.
But what use is a mountain?"

Dark clouds hang heavy on the peaks
majestic, threatening, foreboding.

*In the west
a pale sun silently descends beneath the earth
a dazzling ray of light
    slices a brilliant path
    through inky skies
triumphant note to a grandiose finale.
And when the curtain falls on this performance,
the unseen presence of the peaks
    lingers in the night
    like the ghost of a powerful god.*

*The real question is:
    what use is she for this mountain?*

Forest

I walk alone in a forest
where graceful trembling aspen
reach for the sky.

I love the silence
broken only by the chirping of squirrels
perfumed by wild strawberries
nestling
among leaves covered in sparkling morning dew.

The cry of a solitary loon
sliding along the mirror of a hidden lake
                      breaks the silence.

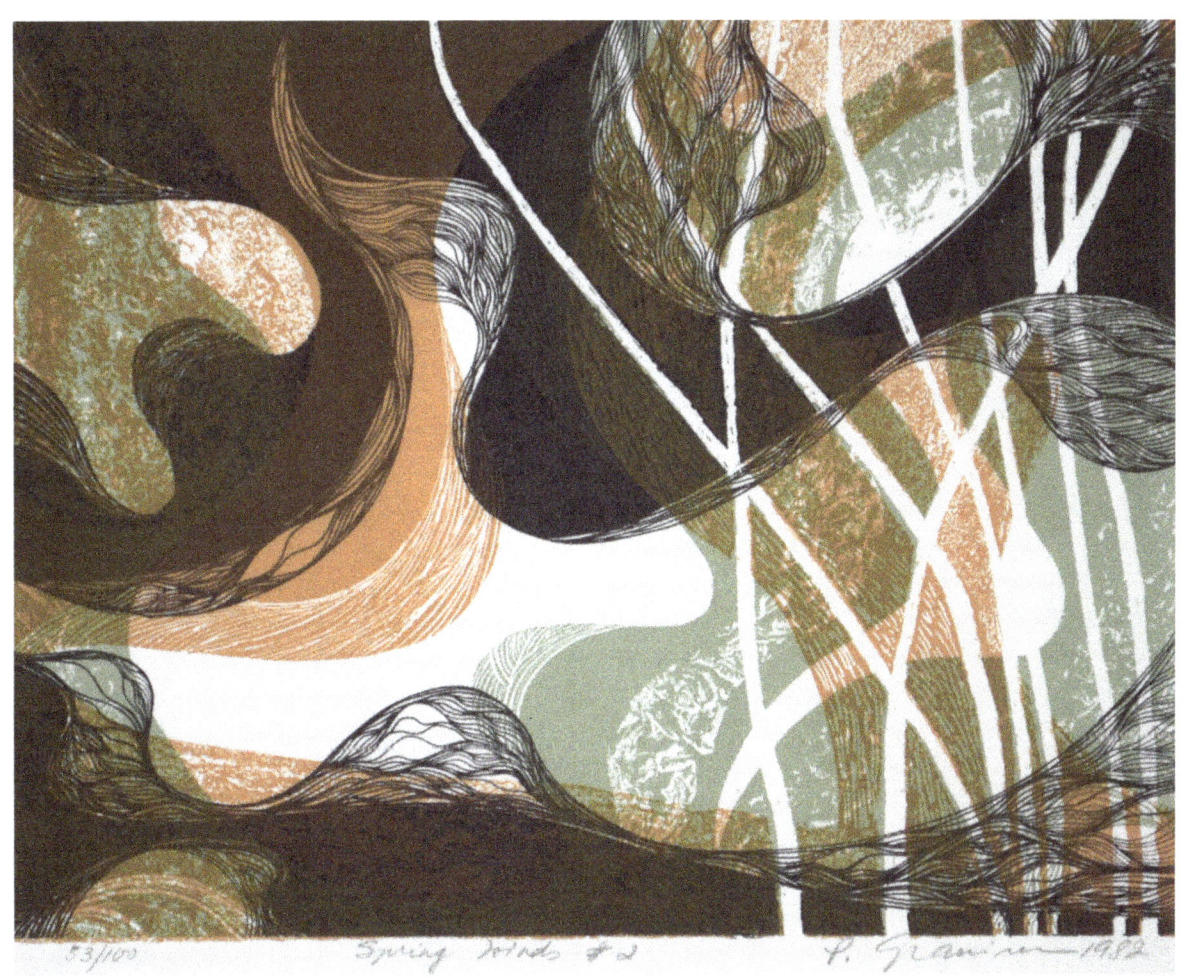

Spring Winds 2, 1982, silk screen, 7×9 in.

Journal Notes

Hot day again.

Picked some wild strawberries.

The lake was gorgeous this evening
water like a mirror
with lovely pastel pinks and blues
elegant gold-lined cloud formations
like ghosts of ancient gods.

Today I did a painting that worked!

Emma Lake Artists' Retreat, Saskatchewan, July 18, 1989

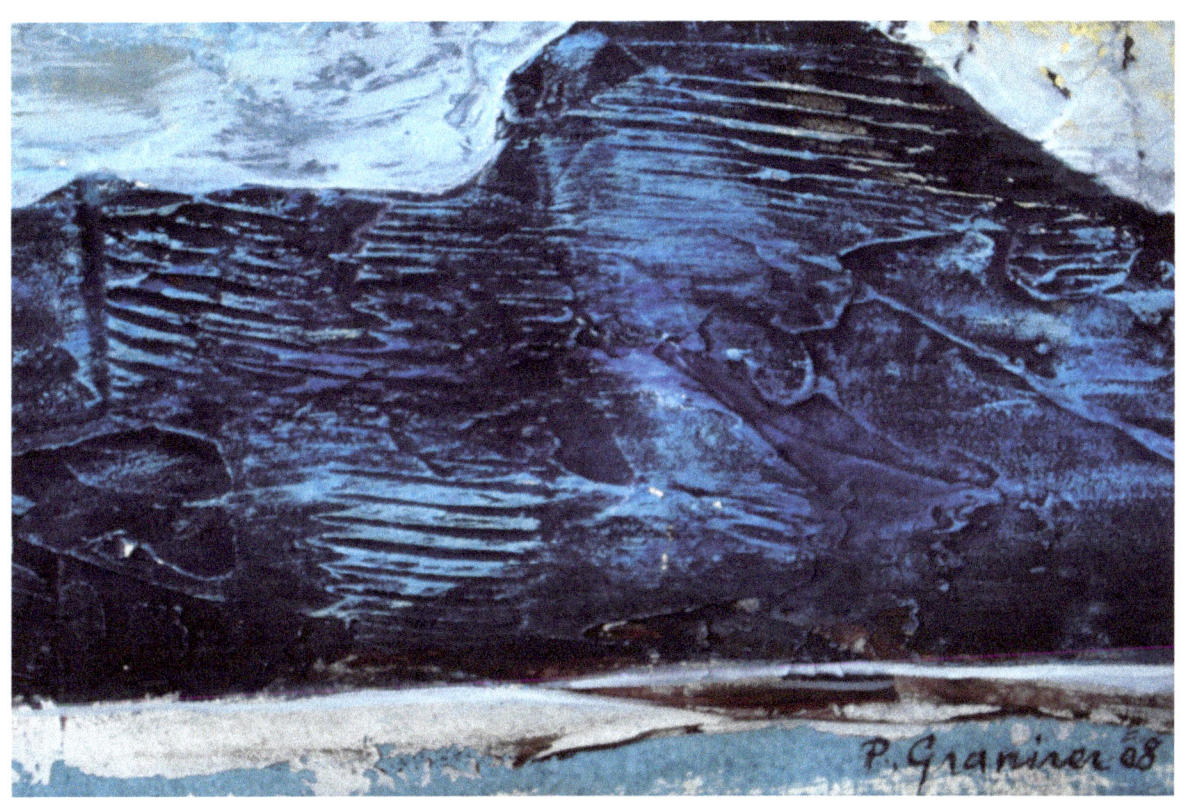

Mountain, 2008, mixed media on paper, 4×6 in.

Meditation in a Zen Garden

War
is raging
in the hot Arabian sands.

But here in this garden
the sand is silvery and cool
raked patterns smooth and even.

Silent stones
oasis
of peaceful meditation
distant and protected.

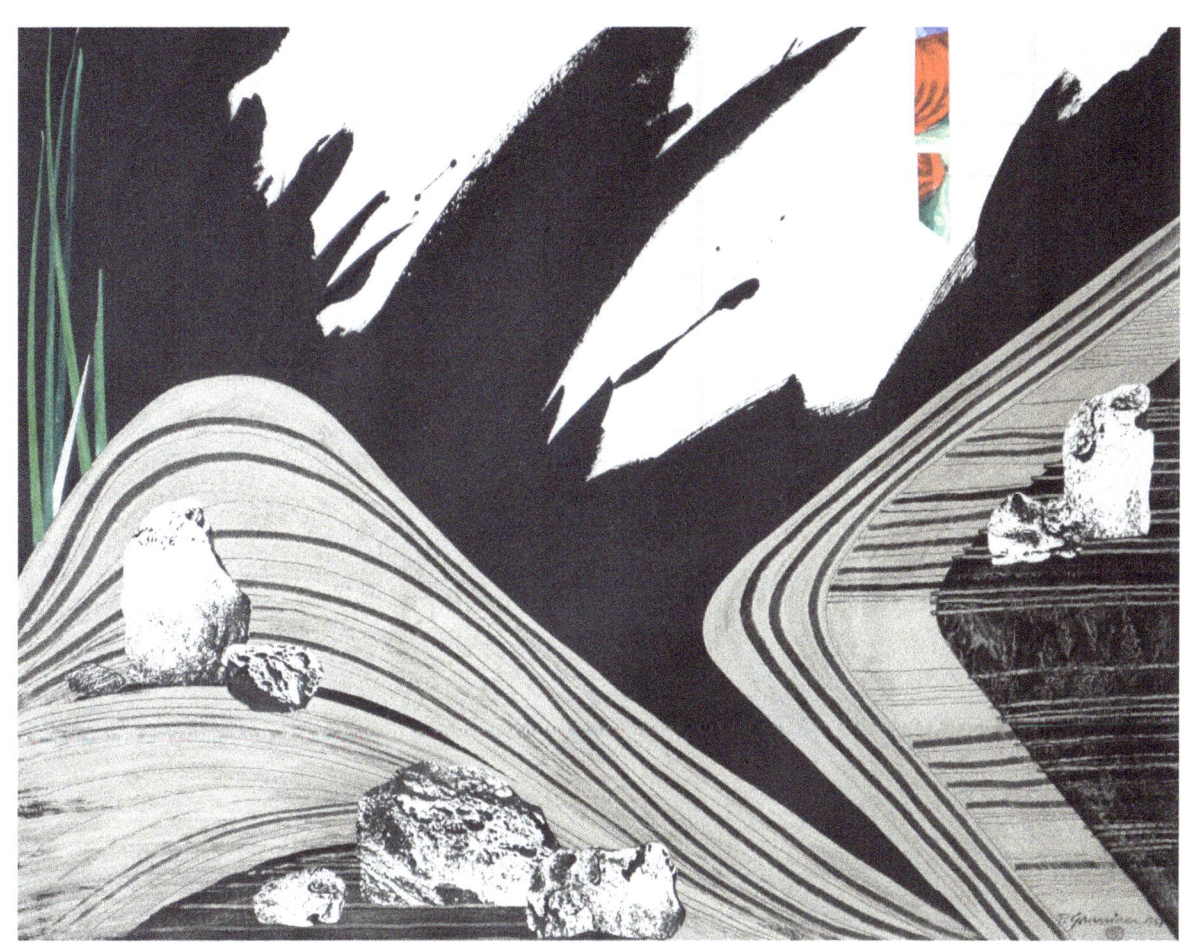
Sand Garden, 1991, mixed media on paper, 22×30 in.

Pas-de-deux

Green blanket spread along the golden sand
sailboats, whitecaps and blue mountains.
A perfect picture postcard
    for tourists to send home.
People stroll
they jog and bike,
they talk, hold hands and smile at one another
or simply stop and gaze in disbelief
at the Edenic sight.
Splashed on the canvas of a perfect sky
a pair of kites soar high above the grassy knoll
black and red and white and yellow —
paper birds held prisoner by slender threads.
Holding fast
onto taut strings,
two men stand close together, one kite for each.
They leap
    they dance
        they bend and kneel
           they sway from side to side
and turn as one.

The kites race up and down
and left and right
a mighty pas-de-deux
danced to the roaring of the wind.
The men move swiftly, drunk with power
like gods ruling the heavens.

But soon —
      the show is over.
The kites fall from the sky
      a lifeless
         pile of colour on the grass.

The men, spent
and ordinary now
slowly move apart and shyly smile.

There is scattered applause from the small gathered crowd.

Red

Red splashes in the grass,
poppies drunk with sunshine
satin petals
smooth as silk
black seeds hidden
deep in their heart.

I dip my brush in paint
    red as blood
    red as shiny cranberries
    red as the pointed roof
on the house next door
    red on my empty canvas.

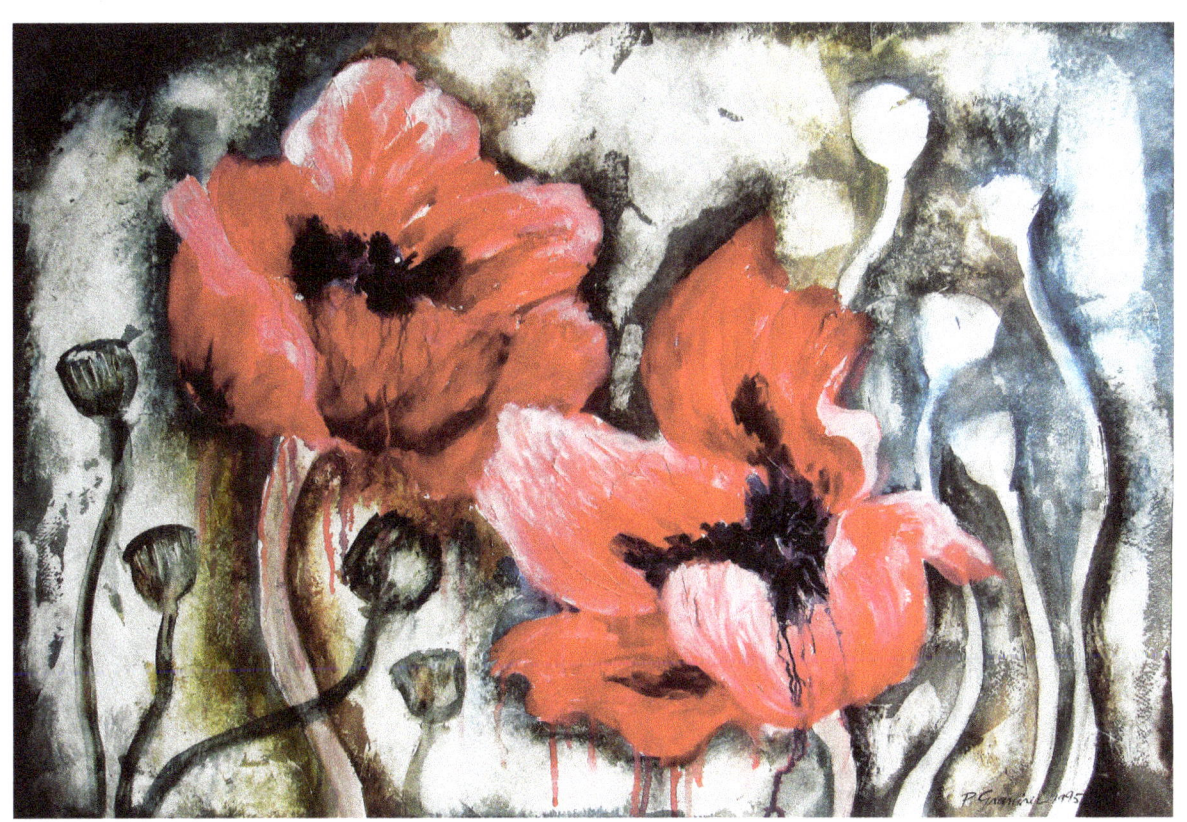

Poppies with Pods, 1995, mixed media on paper, 27×39 in.

Marjorie

She panics
when she leaves New York.
The open sky, the far horizon
the fields, the trees, the mountains
　　　　　　　all frighten her.
Fresh air gives her headaches
nature terrifies her.
The City is her cradle
her habitat
her smoggy and familiar surroundings.

Should I
like any zealous missionary
try to convert her
and bring her back to Eden?
Should I take her hand
and gently lead her to these rugged shores,
let her hear the rhythm of the waves,
and the sharp cries of seagulls dancing in the wind?
Will she be able to overcome her fear of the gods
whose footprints still linger on the sand?

God

Worship houses
    churches
        mosques
            and synagogues.
People kneel and bow and pray for help
    from a powerful, imagined God.

This deity, the One and Only God
it has three names
    at least.

Is Adonai the father
    of Jesus Christ
        or has he changed his name
            to Allah?
Perhaps it's just a case
    of personality disorder?

This God, the Ruler of the Universe
Is powerless to stop the humans
from killing one another
in His many names.

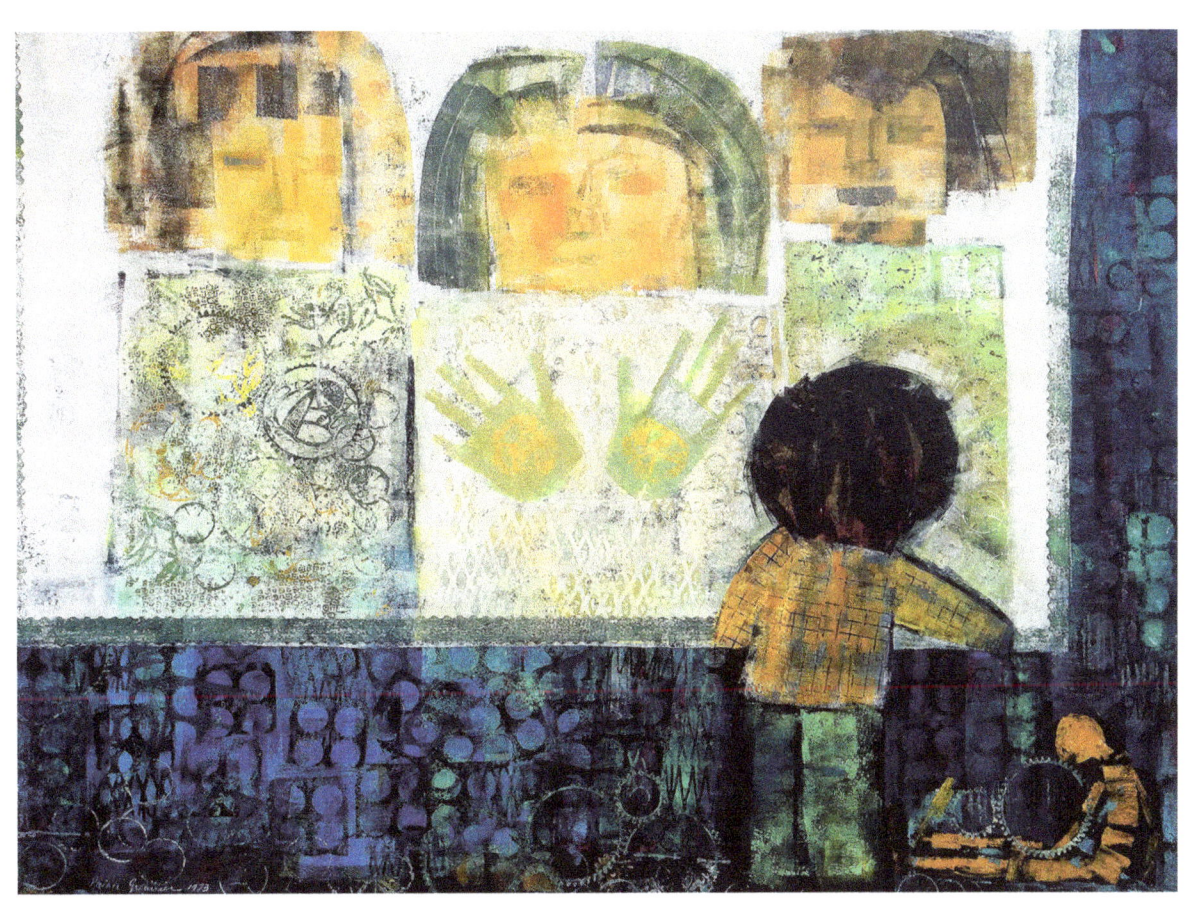

A Child's Fantasy, 1973, mixed media on card, 28×36 in.

Questions of Id-Entity

Mirror, mirror on the wall
Do I know myself at all?

A small black ant hurries on the path. Why? Why the rush? What is the urge that keeps it scurrying at such speed? Where does it come from and where is it going?
Another ant appears from the opposite direction. Will they stop to greet one another? Would they recognize each other if they met again?

Do ants have identities?

The sky darkens as a murder of crows, wings flapping, their shrieking resonating through the quiet evening in a cacophony of raucous sound, fly over the trees. Is this a date? How do they know the time to meet?

Do crows have identities?

Consider the lion, look at the elephant, watch the apes, the dogs, the cats; they know, they feel, they understand, they love, they mourn. They do have identities.

And us humans, the jewel in the crown of life's creation, the Masters of the Universe? Are we alone, each with our unique identity?

But in a crowd, a herd, a mob—would we still have it?

Would I know me in a crowd? Who am I and why am I here? Have I become just a grain of sand in a raging sandstorm?

Migration

As immigrants, our roots severed, held only by unreliable memories, has our identity been abandoned in the country we left behind? Who are we now?

Dislocation

How deep will our new roots be? Will we acquire a new culture like the octopus that grows a new arm? Where do we come from?

Relocation

When growing roots in a new country, what will be left of the old?

Will our identity be like a pack of cards kept tight together in our brain, to be tossed as needed on the table of our life?

A card for each language acquired, a card for each event experienced, a card for events remembered, cards for love of family, joys of friendship and sorrow of loss.

Where do I come from—who am I—where am I going?

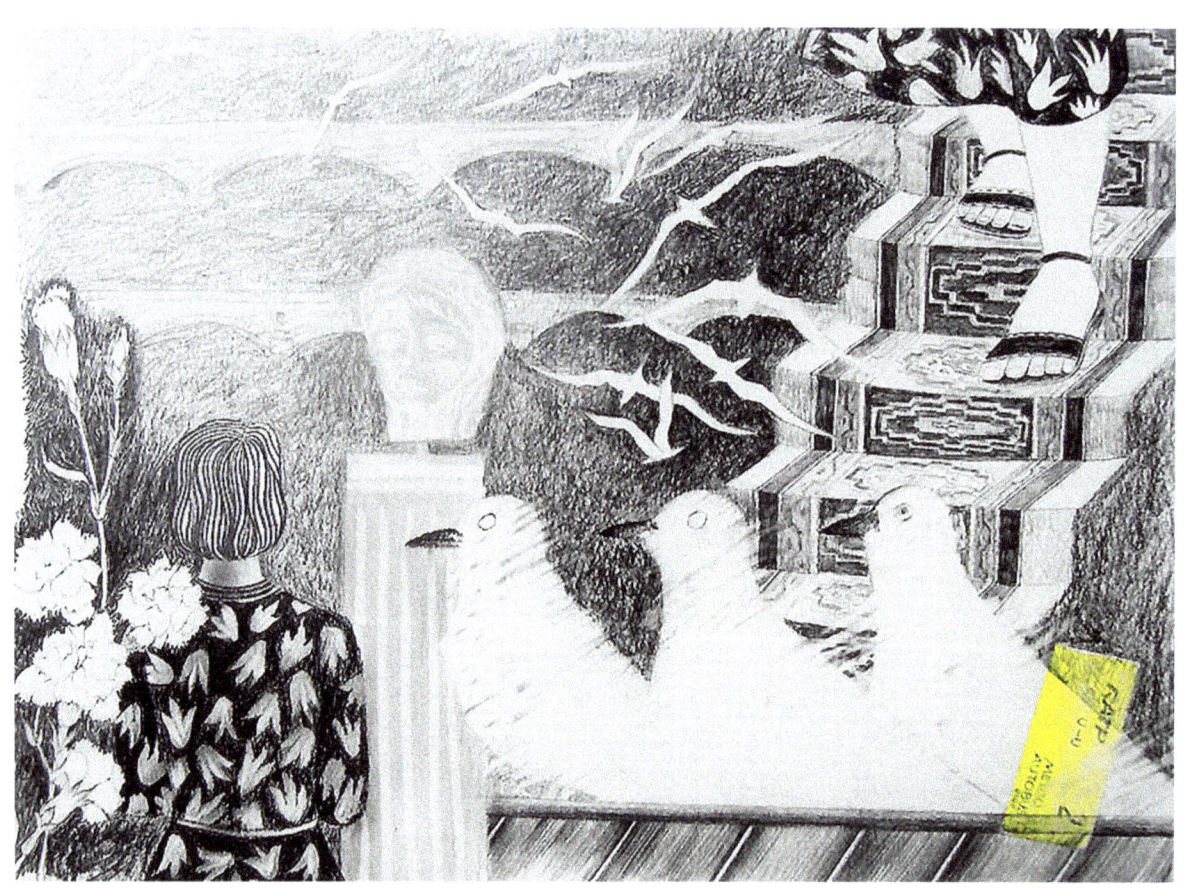
Dream, 1987, graphite on paper, collage, 7×9 in.

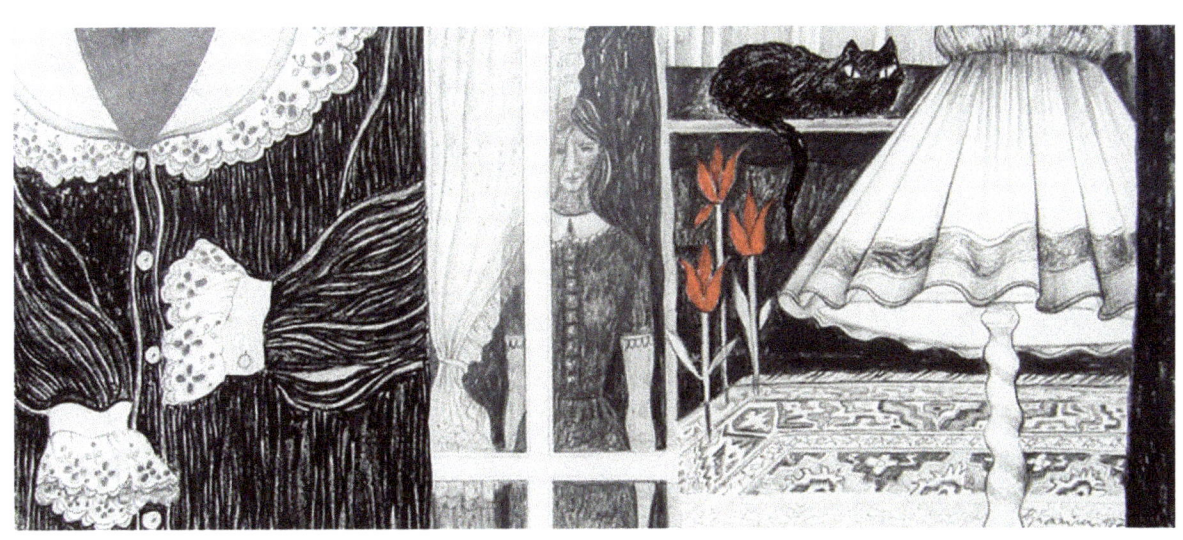
Lausanne Reverie, 1987, graphite and pencil on paper, 7×14 in.

Closure

Goodbye

after 66 years together

It's time . . .

the nurse's words
hover in the still night
float through the open door
      a fluttering of wings
      a wounded bird.

It's time.

Weak pulse struggles against my fingers —
don't stop, don't stop.
His tired eyes are closed.

Does he see my anxious face?
Does he feel
      my kiss on his pale forehead
      does he feel my closeness
      does he feel my love?

It's time, my dear one

                                goodbye . . .

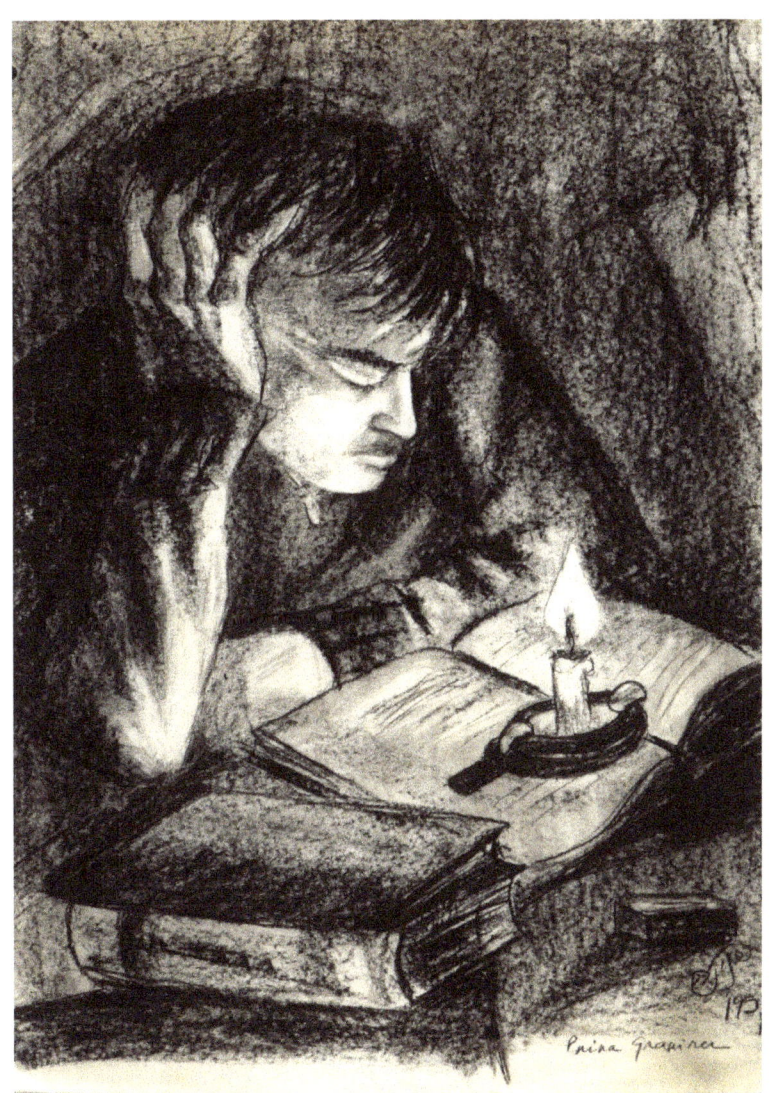

Eddy studying during power outage, 1957, charcoal on paper, 25×18 in.

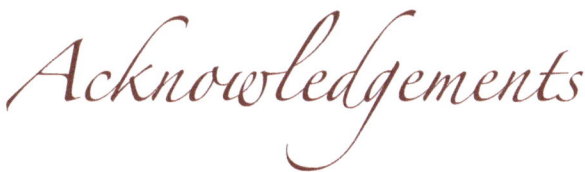

Acknowledgements

A writer's words are written in silence; they come to life only when a reader's eyes travel over the printed page. I have been fortunate to have family and friends who encouraged me to continue on the journey of assembling these small poems written over a lifetime, so that others may enjoy them.

Many thanks to my dear friends Linda Shulman, Nurit Fox, Ketty Magill, Jan Smith, Maureen Chacon, Sidi Schaffer, Jeanne Krabbendam and Selina Chew, who en-couraged me when I wavered.

Graham Good, Phyllis Reeve and Lillian Boraks-Nemetz gave me some tough love; their assistance with editing helped me avoid a few embarrassing mistakes.

I was particularly touched by the enthusiasm shown by my sons David and Dan, and my daughter-in-law Beatrice. Many thanks to Aislinn Cottell for her much needed help in bringing this project to completion. And it was a real pleasure to work again with publisher Jo Blackmore, editor Kyle Hawke and book designer Omar Gallegos, who showed endless patience with my many changes.

And last, but most importantly, my deepest thanks to my artist friend Janet Lee, without whom the high resolution photography would never have happened.

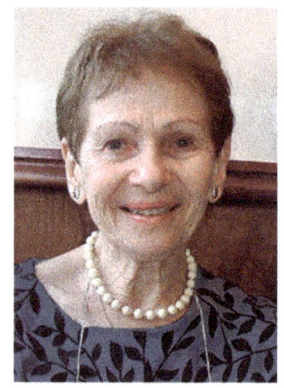

Pnina Granirer was born in Romania and immigrated to Israel in 1950. She studied at the Bezalel Art Academy in Jerusalem and came to Canada in 1965, settling in Vancouver where she has lived ever since. Her works are displayed in private and public galleries and museum collections in Canada, the US, Chile, Europe and Israel. An extensive archive of documentation on her work and life can be found in the British Columbia Artists' Archives at the University of Victoria, BC.

Granirer has always followed her own vision, taking risks by disregarding the trends and fashions of the art world. In 1993 Granirer co-founded Artists in Our Midst, the first annual Studio Tour in Vancouver, BC. For six years she organized and hosted discussions about art via Philosopher Art Cafes sponsored by Simon Fraser University. She has been featured in several films, including Pnina Granirer: *Profile of an Artist* (1989) and *The Trials of Eve* (1992).

In 2014 the artist was included in the encyclopedia of International Surrealism by Arturo Schwarz, *Il Surrealismo—Ieri e Oggi* (Italy) and in a five-page chapter of José Miguel Pérez Corrales's Anthology, *Surrealismo: El Oro del Tiempo* (Spain).

A visual artist for over 60 years, Granirer has also written verse since her childhood. *Garden of Words* contains musings that both reflect and illuminate her paintings. The sculpted stones in the Gulf Islands, the joy of watching dancers' bodies in movement, the shadow of a new plague, and the contemplation of being human in a complex world—all are an expression of Granirer's wish "to plant a garden of words in [her] field of colours."

You're invited to visit her website:

www.pninagranirer.com

www.ingramcontent.com/pod-product-compliance
Lightning Source LLC
Chambersburg PA
CBHW040543220526
45473CB00016B/3004